rhythms primeval

poems
by
Maya Mitra Das

Azalea Art Press
Berkeley . California

**© Maya Mitra Das, 2017.
All Rights Reserved.**

ISBN: 978-1-943471-21-8

Cover Art
& Interior Paintings:
Patti Edmon
http://pattiedmon.blogspot.com

Dedication

I dedicate this book to Dr. Jerry Ball—poet, actor, dramatist and instructor of philosophy, humanities and religion.

I first met Jerry in a class where he introduced us to the world of opera. He encouraged me to join his poetry class, promising that he would guide me to write in this new genre. I was very skeptical and nervous, but at that moment I entered a wonderland of inspiration from which, as Jerry would say, "there is no escape." He has truly been my writing guru.

Dr. Ball has received many awards, including three grand prizes for haiku awarded by the Yuki Teikei Haiku Society of Canada and the United States. He has published several books of verse and haiku, and co-edited the *San Francisco Haiku Anthology*.

Other Titles by Maya Mitra Das

Silhouettes of Time / 2016
Intriguing tales bring the reader on highly
imaginative journeys through time, space and memory.

**Tremors:
Short Fiction by California Authors / 2014**
A collection of soul-stirring contemporary fiction
by eight San Francisco Bay Area authors.

Contents

Introduction by Jerry Ball ... i

I.

Dancing Fireflies ... 3
Desolate Place ... 4
My Friend ... 5
A Meteor of a Burning Hear ... 6
A Bouquet of Foam ... 7
The Noiseless World ... 8
Journey to a Dark Land ... 9
The Waves ... 10
Despair ... 11
Fire ... 12
We Bow to Shiva ... 13
Last of the Evening ... 14

II.

Haiku ... 17

III.

Muse ... 23
An Echo of Rahma: A Historical Tale ... 26
The Magic of Imagination ... 30
The Last Cadence ... 33
The Chain of Pearls ... 34
Sunrise Over Kachanjhunga ... 35
The Harvest Moon ... 36

IV.

Haiku   41

V.

The Brook	47
Morning	48
A Day	49
Maple Leaves	50
The Dark	51
The Winter Arrives	52
The Moon	53
Lost Dream	54
To Keats	55
Last Sunset of the Year	56
Acknowledgements	*59*
About the Author	*61*
Contact/Book Orders	*62*

Introduction

I'm very happy to write a brief introduction to Maya Mitra Das's new book of poems.

Maya has been a writing student of mine for the past five years, during which sometimes it has been difficult to determine who is the student and who is the teacher. With the present book, that job is no easier.

As a writer, Maya exemplifies a unique set of characteristics. She is multi-cultural and multi-lingual. She is well-read in history and well-versed in many cultures. She is a dancer and experienced in collaborating with artists and inspiring others.

Maya trained as a hematologist and this is also combined with good common sense. Though Maya has considerable analytical skills, she knows when to stop being analytical. She is able to understand and express the differences between a scientific and a poetic view of the world.

The result of this combination is unique, as you will see when you read this engaging and insightful collection.

- Dr. Jerry Ball
February 2017

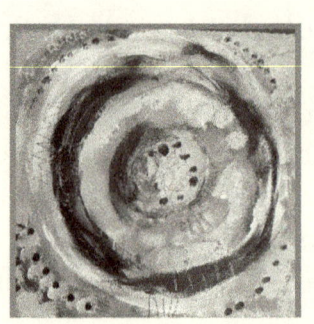

rhythms primeval

I.

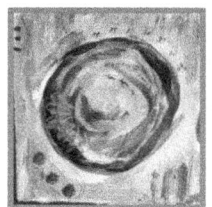 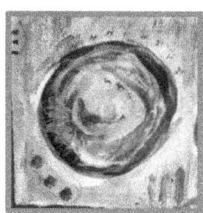 

Dancing Fireflies

Over the valley
where the mountain meets
the swaying paddy fields

To where the light veil of evening
spreads over the ridge
the red moon is an oblong disk

People gather to dance above the dwellings
crickets serenade and owls begin their hooting refrain
night becomes a darkened stage

Where
to the beat of muffled drums
the fireflies dance madly

Desolate Place

On the slope of
a lonely stream
I sit on the edge and
muse on this desolate place

Here the melodies of solitude
breeze through tall grasses
and shadows chase the light
all day

My Friend

The profound quiet of the day
changes slowly to evening's gray
as silence wraps about me like a viper

'Oh, no!' I want to scream
words trickle forth, but get lost
I remain silent

From the dark landscape
crickets chirp incessantly
the murmuring brook never stops

Night birds shrill the air
rising moon bathes the earth
in magnificent beams

Light and shade
I embrace my friend
my dear Loneliness

A Meteor of a Burning Heart

A meteor of a burning heart
shoots across the dark sky

When curtains of eyes are raised high
searching for a stage within or without

They find a symbol of wholeness
inside the bottom of deep darkness

The search ends in partial fulfillment
through a sacrifice on an altar of devotion

That shines, in part, in wholeness
and finds its wholeness in parts

A Bouquet of Foam

A long way off, in rolls rain
from a mountainous terrain

Washed with falls, and bathed
in ocean, arriving lonely, searching
for something, with knowledge of nothing

Among so many blues
eyes confused to catch the hues
dark, heavenly and sunken colors
clusters form with grace of wind

Nothing is here but light in clusters
then it offers us its final secret

A search not in vain
my gift—a bouquet of foam

The Noiseless World

Noises soft and loud pierce our ears
noises like thunder rise up high

Noises like an agony
break one's heart

Noises a wave of sound
in melodious disguise

Yet I contemplate a noiseless world
where imagery thrives

And I catch a glimpse
of this vibrant universe

Journey to a Dark Land

I journey to a dark land where
neither moon nor stars shine
there, angry storms roll in
chariot and lash the light
trees huddle in fear and whisper

While the withered leaves rustle
their moaning songs
I ride to the dark land
no more fear in my mind

In the spiral of darkness
I find my sorrow waiting
waiting to be
absolutely, absolutely mine

The Waves

Waves like fanned out snakes
keep crashing on solemn rocks

Sun's last kiss of the day
spills color in a glorious way

Of all waves big and small
I love but only one

The wave that came very close
and touched me with a shiver

Set my silhouette on sand to tremor
then dissolved in wavy quiver

I cry out loud and utter
"Is this your message?"

Seagull shrieks and ocean rumbles

Despair

It shoves and hurts
within the soul resides

And so my spirit wonders
whence the surge?

Fire

On a winter day in Suisun,
I escape from a misty landscape
entering a room with a well-lit fireplace

The flickering flames emanating glow
make dancing Shiva's radiance show
"Touch me!" I cry out loud

"Touch me with the primeval rhythm
of the cosmos, the dance of the constellations
and the stars, the far-flung fireballs"

With the veil of time I bow to Thee
grant me the fire I can hold inside me
and burn the veil to eternity

We Bow to Shiva

We bow to Shiva
The Lord of Dances
between the rehearsal
and performances

The sounds echo
Ta Dhi Ge Na Tom
my heart beats faster
and feet quaver

Possessed with
primeval rhythm
I enter the stage
with waves of motion

Ta Dhi Ge Na tom
Ta Dhi N Ge Na Tom
I mingle with infinite energy
and time flows endlessly

Last of the Evening

Standing by the window
in the last of the evening
two stars glare down
through the ribs of clouds

Then the red moon ascends
to smear the hills with hazy dreams
a sudden blast of cold breeze
rumbles through the shivering trees

The cold blast and foggy veil
makes my heart sink
in the deep of a dark abyss
the still deepens but rolls along

Swaying shadows whisper
"Not here, not here"
my thoughts float up
my vision goes far

Over the moon struck hills
and far beyond
my heart undisturbed
slowly settles in peaceful calm

II.

 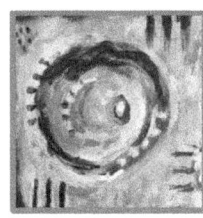 

Dew drops are falling
Startled daisies open eyes
Sun hides, bids goodbye

Around meadow
River of mist flows
Across the evening dark

A tiny sparrow hops
On wet green grasses
Autumn's first rain

Moon's misty veil
Spreads over hill and dale
Shadows of whispering trees

The Autumn breeze
Calls for the leaves
I hug my loneliness

Moon nearly full but moist
Slopes of the mountain wrapped in shades
Stand silently: a dark wall

Fall spills its color
Over valleys trees whisper
Adieu, adieu

Autumn wind dances
Through branches of oak tree
Wind chimes start its melody

Rain chatters through trees
Camellias welcome the festivity
Cry of birds breaks the peace

III.

Muse

The pine trees stand at the end of my deck
several grouped together: I love them
one is close enough
for the touch of my hand

The trees stand tall enough to touch the sky
on autumn mornings
dew hangs like pearls
read to drop

Misty rays of sun
struggle through branches
framing Mt. Diablo, the Devil Mountain
cloaked in green

Solemn witness to morning ritual
one Tree stands over me in prayer, in search for peace
I am safely sheltered by its dark brown trunk
and fresh needles of bright green

A shared breakfast with my cockatiel, Samrat
begins with Samrat's musical speech
flowing to and fro with the sighing of the wind
echoing softly in the branches of the trees

Off to Children's Hospital—my workplace
busy list, much to do
quick round of patients
transfusions and chemo infusions

At last the end of day
through stop-and-go traffic, I breathe easy
with the thought of home and yard
welcomed by the joy of my bird and the Tree

Samrat is eager for company after a lonely day
his noisy greeting summons me to open the cage
free at last, he is on my shoulder
planting tender pecks on my cheek

The tea kettle sings a beckoning song
as a cup of tea warms my hands, my tensions melt away
housework fills the quiet evening hours
aware, my tree offers silent support

Late now, the birds and squirrels quietly at rest
the Tree stands tall, awaiting the coming night
I ask for news—*Will it rain again?*
the Tree sways in answer —*Yes, it shall*

Last night's storm
had the Tree dancing in the wind

whistling through branches about the house
playing a lullaby on wind chimes
The Tree watched the house and all who are in it
it sang to me and put all the birds to sleep
I will come again to watch the Tree
at the rising of the moon

We shall share the moonlight
whose light softly brushes
the branches of the Tree
making it dreamy and regal

Stately as it is
guardian of my home and soul
my Tree has merged and fused with me
it sends me to a land beyond a land

What is this? An abstract entity?
no, it is something much more
eternal, primeval, everlasting
Pure love!

It is my muse

An Echo of Rahma: A Historical Tale

I.

Waves of melodies echo from the past
a tune of Bhairabi played by my great grandmother.
her room was on the second floor
with big windows and a marble floor

Born in the late 19th century
olive-skinned Rahma with big black eyes
had many talents: she wrote poetry
and played her clarinet with a regal smile

Looking like a sculpted figure
gold bangles dazzling like stars
I used to call her Bima
fondly she called me Naiyna

II.

She married a young man at sixteen
who was district judge in her home town
in the west part of Bengal
far from the big city of Kolkata

Echoes of tunes from the past
keep on echoing, till this day
Bima was a special woman
co-founded an institute for destitute women

To help the poor, Bima started their work
and brought rupees for their craft,
trained herself in midwifery
and assisted delivering newborn babies

III.

In summer we went on morning rides
often by the riverside
the river Ganges was full to the brink
a steamer whistled and chugged along

While the river flowed elegantly
people on the banks prayed peacefully
the cool breeze and tranquility refreshed us completely
the time to return came all too quickly

One day I wanted a real story
along with cups of tea swirling steam
Bima's eyes sparkled
as she started the story

The sun came out of the clouds
and spilled its color all around
the clouds returned
Bima held her clarinet sadly and began

IV.

When goods of India were banned
clothes from the British Isles took over the market
weaver's thumbs were sacrificed to save their lives
This we must not permit, Bima exclaimed

Bima's eyes searched the distance in agony
an event was organized
a women's group would march to the town square
and burn clothes imported from England

The women of the town gathered
Rahma led the march, right in front
carrying the national flag in her right hand
she shouted, *British quit India!*

The women shouted, *British quit India soon!*
Bande Ma taram (Glory to our Mother)
they marched to the town square in peace
followed closely by police and passersby

At the town square they stopped
clothes from Manchester were gathered
they started a fire in the heap of clothes
flames rose in snake-like smoke filling the sky

V.

Mounted police charged with their batons,
one-by-one women fell to the ground.
lying in the river of blood, they shouted
Please, please leave our town!

Bima, with a fractured arm, bleeding forehead
held her flag up, screaming, *Leave our land!*
the news spread like wildfire from one town to another
until the British monopoly ceased

VI.

Wind chimes play gently
the setting sun spills its color of glory
the evening's darkness spreads the veil
while crickets start their serenade

While stars twinkle one by one
the sound of the *Raga* keeps on coming
the tune of Bhairabi that was played
by my great grandmother

The Magic of Imagination

Two little girls started playing
at the sloping backyard of a bungalow
down at the bottom, the river Murri was still flowing
but very shallow at this time of year

Like it was yesterday I can see the bungalow
the river, the big rocky isles in the middle of the river
and beyond the rocky isle the sandy isles with shrubs
where the birds are hopping and chirping

I can see myself whispering to my friend, Prititi
Prititi, look! That rock in the middle is the gate of a castle
What do you mean Mita? Tell me, tell me!
Listen, and you will hear the story

If this rock in the middle of the river was the gate
then there was a bridge
used to open or close by the men who were guards at the gate
far away, the hill was the big castle

What?
Listen, inside the castle there was a prince
and his dear friend, like you and me
Prititi's eyes were wide open
Then what happened?

*They are all under a spell
and cursed by a wicked witch
Why?
Why? She is the wicked witch isn't she?*

*Oh I am sad, is he a good prince?
Yes, he is and he is a good looking brave prince
Then, why didn't he do anything?
The wicked witch threw a spell, and he and all others fell asleep*

*What are we going to do?
We are going to go there and save them
You mean you and me!
Yes, are you ready?
How? It is far*

*We are going to fly with two horses, with wings
What color, I want white.
I want white too.
Now close your eyes and say
'Anga Banga Hing Ring Phat'*

We were on our imaginary horses
and I just warned Prititi that we have to fight bravely
to save the prince and his dear friend
when I heard my mom calling, *Prititi's mother is here!*

Five more minutes, please, I replied
Five more minutes only? said Prititi
We cannot do this in five minutes!
Okay then, the Prince, his friend and the people have to wait for us

Prince charming or not we got our life partners
Prititi married an Air Force marshall
she travels around India
wherever her husband is stationed

I found myself at present cruising across the sky
with my fellow doctors to Estonia
down below were white and black clouds
heaped up like mounds of huge cotton balls

I got lost in my past
I could see so clearly the little Bungalow
the backyard slope to the shallow river
the chirping birds and two little playful girls

On winged white horses
In search of their princes

The Last Cadence

Adriana in a long flowing dress
walked through the meadow in the afternoon
the meadow looked like a painting in yellow
large and small daisies swaying gently with the breeze

The fresh smell of grass
was both enchanting and bothersome
the pollen made Adriana start to sneeze
she thought to return, but at that moment
she saw in the distance an outline near the water
like a mirage

She saw what looked like a man
kneeling very close to a tree near the water
It cannot be, she gasped, moving closer
the man's feet hovered above the ground

She screamed
the man hung there helplessly, a rope around his neck
his drooping arms swaying in rhythm with the breeze
eyes fixed gazing towards the infinite
expressionless, with no light

It seemed his voiceless melody traveled far away
Adriana stared at him, frozen with fear
her body suddenly swaying in tandem with his
the grasses writhing like spirits in the spring breeze

The Chain of Pearls

Black clouds grace the sky
as a veil of dark falls below
the breeze is sighing by

Tearful mothers' wailing eyes
drip as rain drips
as their sons' blood rolls in the ocean

Mothers, I can only weave
a chain of pearls
with my tears of sorrow

A chain of pearls
around thy neck
with tears of my sorrow

Sunrise Over Kachanjhunga

One chilly October at three in the morning
we board our station wagon

The wagon attempts a slow ascent
followed by a rapid descent

As we move forward
the sheet of darkness moves backward

The winding path suddenly narrows
making one wheel hang dangerously out over the road

We reach the famous Tiger Hill
to see the sun's colorful spill

Clouds and fog passing close
makes one feel damp and cold

Behind the peaks of Kachanjunga
the rays of sun play their overture

The spectrum of colors is all over
trapped and floating on the river of light

The birds chirp and pine forest murmurs
mountain sings to the glory of the nature

The peaks of Kanchanjugha with sprinkled alchemy
make time stop, and move to eternity

The Harvest Moon

Summer was shy
to say goodbye

The harvest moon was up
filling the sky

The trees swayed
in the gentle breeze

Murmuring their songs
to a misty dream

The moon like a
baked round loaf

Peeped through the
drifting clouds

Over the moonstruck land
along with hoots of owls

I traveled back in time
to a faraway place

Landing on a moon-brushed house
in an old, familiar courtyard

Yes, here! Yes, here!
Under the harvest moon

I played and danced
I danced and played

with my loving Grandmother
all the way until the dawn

IV.

 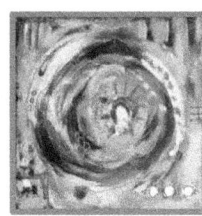 

Horizon merges in mist
Evening spreads the veil
Thoughts empty in silence

Shadows darken
In the mountain canyons framed
In pine branches

Autumn breeze
The fallen leaves in the shadow
Still rustling

A thousand diamonds
Raindrops on oak leaves
In the haze of wintry sun

Through the quiet
The Rocky River comes closer
With rounded softness

Autumn afternoon
Misty light slants through trees
Sudden thunder breaks the peace

Misty morning
Dreamy landscape blushed
First kiss of sun

Rain drops falling
From the slender leaves of tall grasses
At the foot of the mountain

In winter rain
A pool where two muddy streams meet
A green frog jumps

V.

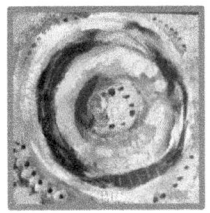 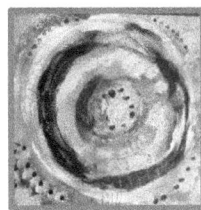 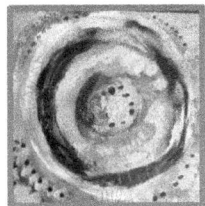

The Brook

Life runs busy with affairs
brook runs busy with water

Days in life slide and glide
brook slips, slides, dances and glides

Life with no escape, dances alone
brook hides and hums along

Then bursts with joy, murmurs its song

Morning

In morning's soft glow
I open my eyes
a little bird sings
get up and hurry
why hurry?
why?

I feed the wild birds
I fill the plate
with a sense of pleasure
I see the birds hop
to the plate with joy
they turn and twist
oh, what a sight to see
I could dance and hop
with equal glee

Here comes the squirrel
in his morning vigor
with puffed up tail
he shows his power
I chase the squirrel off the plate
what a shame the birds fly off

And all my work in vain

A Day

The morning silence breaks
with songs of birds
dreamy moon cruises along the sky
orange gold pierces the rift of cloud
winter wind blows its horn aloud

Roadside grass with frosty head
trembles quietly colored in red
welcoming the day, daisies bow gently
with no heed we pass
on our way to our busy day

Maple Leaves

The last glow of sun
covers the mountains

A cool autumn breeze
shivers the maple trees

Twisting and turning
leaves keep falling

Resting on the ground
they cast their last glance up at the tree

Once they were
where they belong

Now, startled by a cool breeze
leaves hurdle together

With a sigh they murmur
Adieu! No more fear!

The Dark

Winter blows its horn
ghostly trees shiver and mourn

Afternoon light fades
evening slowly spreads

Loving fight of light and dark
ends only in dark

The dark grows and gathers
trees coldly whisper

"The eternal silence"
in dark and in cold

A soul searches the tragic
the beauty and the magic

Of longing, to be loved
and through Love
makes its secrets known

The Winter Arrives

The winter arrives silently
mist wraps trees
when wind blows gently

The silence that falls
all night from the stars
becomes a song

The song that swells
in melodies in the sea
surges up, all day playfully

Now evening has come
down on shore in fading light
the seabirds follow
the song to their warm nests

The Moon

Mist flows over the valleys, mist rolls over the hills
mist wraps around the shadowy trees

Moon breaks through the clouds
spreads its veil over the lonely path

With the moon casting a shadow as my friend
I make my way back slowly through the dark

Lost Dream

The sky is overcast with clouds
the rain is ceaseless
winter is here, at my door

Moments of lightning
cast down a darker gloom
my heart gropes in the dark

For the lost dream
dives in a deep void
to find my tryst

My tryst! My tryst!
who else, who else?

Deep in the void
it is me
it is me
it is me

To Keats

Under Rome's blue sky
lay the Piazza di Spagna

Blossoms, ruins, statues and music
glories all that infused into the poet Hyperion

Who grew like a pale flower
and ended in complete despair

Keats was truly like Shakespeare
a being of complete and spontaneous utterance

A poet
a prophet

Last Sunset of the Year

The last sunset of the year
kisses the Earth goodbye
and changes the color of all things

Standing alone
I start counting the forgotten dreams

Figures disappear into the fog
and their footfalls muffle
in the breeze

Shivers of winter shake me up
I dive in the deep unconscious

Finding dreams I left behind
I start again to weave my life
standing alone in a misty screen

Of my imaginings

Acknowledgements

My thanks to Karen Mireau for publishing this book. Her creative guidance, support and communication have been invaluable.

I am grateful to Sharon Stewart for encouraging me to publish these poems and Janice De Jesus for her ongoing help and inspiration.

My appreciation also to abstract artist Patti Edmon, whose images grace the cover and interior of this book.

Last, but not least, I thank my writing classmates—their constant input provided the motivation to improve and refine these poems and has been instrumental to me in becoming a better writer.

Maya Mitra Das

About the Author

Poet and short story writer Maya Mitra Das was born in India and came to the U.S. in 1973. She studied internal medicine and pediatrics in India, England and the United States, earning her M.D. and Ph.D. She received her training at Downstate Medical Center and State University Hospital in Brooklyn, New York.

She completed two fellowships—one for the department of hematology and oncology at U.C.L.A. Medical Center and the second at University of California San Francisco for radiation oncology. She currently serves on the medical staff at Children's Hospital in Oakland, California working with sickle cell anemia in children.

Among her many hobbies, Maya performs 'Bharatnatyam' Indian classical dance. Her poetry has appeared in *Tuesday's Poetry*, edited by Jerry Ball, two narrative poems have been anthologized in *What's in a Name*, edited by Elaine Starkman, and she has also authored several scientific publications. Her fiction has appeared in *Tremors: Short Fiction by California Writers* and in her full-length collection of short stories, *Silhouettes of Time*.

This poetry collection by Maya Mitra Das
may be ordered directly at www.lulu.com.

azaleaartpress.blogspot.com

Azalea.Art.Press@gmail.com

To schedule an interview or signing with the author,
please contact the publisher.

www.ingramcontent.com/pod-product-compliance
Lightning Source LLC
Chambersburg PA
CBHW021025090426
42738CB00007B/908